Music From The Romantic
Musik der Romantik

First Recital Pieces for
Violin & Piano
Erste Spielstücke für Violine und Klavier

Grades One to Three

Edited with interpretative notes
by Elizabeth Turnbull

Herausgegeben mit kurzen Spielanweisungen von Elizabeth Turnbull

BOSWORTH

Music settings by Stave Origination
German translation by Dietmar Fratz
Series cover design by Miranda Harvey
Cover picture: *The Duet* (mezzotint), Karl Schweninger (1818-87)
Stapleton Collection, UK/Bridgeman Art Library

ISMN: M 2016-4057-0

© 2000 Bosworth & Co. Ltd.
Published in Great Britain by Bosworth & Company Ltd.

Head office: 14/15 Berners Street,
London W1T 3LJ

Sales and Hire:
Music Sales Distribution Centre,
Newmarket Road,
Bury St. Edmunds
Suffolk IP33 3YB

Tel +44 (0)1284 702600
Fax + 44 (0)1284 768301

www.musicsales.com
e-mail: music@musicsales.co.uk

Contents

FIRST RECITAL PIECES FOR VIOLIN & PIANO

Erste Spielstücke für Violine und Klavier

A ma chère petite Olga

Chanson de Berceau
(I. - III.)

FELIX BOROWSKI

Rondo

(I. [or III.])

OSKAR RIEDING
Op.22 No.3

Tarantella

(I. - III.)

FRANTIŠEK DRDLA
Op27 No.2

Five Miniatures

(I. [or III.])

1. Polonaise

LUDWIG MENDELSSOHN
Op.11

FINE

Dal segno al fine

2. Little Waltz
Kleiner Waltzer

28

3. March

Soldatenmarsch

4. Cavatina

Dal segno al coda

5. Mosquito Dance

Mückentanz

FINE

Da capo al fine

Czardas
(I. - III.)

GUSTAV HILLE

Da capo al fine

Minuet

(I. & III.)

LUIGI BOCCHERINI
Op. 13, No.5
arranged by Emil Kross

Da capo al fine